WHAT EATS WHAT IN AN OCEAN FOOD CHAIN

WRITTEN BY **SUZANNE SLADE**
ILLUSTRATED BY **ZACK MCLAUGHLIN**

PICTURE WINDOW BOOKS
a capstone imprint

Colorful corals, fish, and plants live together in the oceans. They are all part of food chains. Energy in a food chain is passed from one living thing to the next.

Most food chains rely on the sun. Rays of sun shine through the waves to reach the plants and animals below.

Bright corals live on the ocean floor.
Together their skeletons form a coral reef.

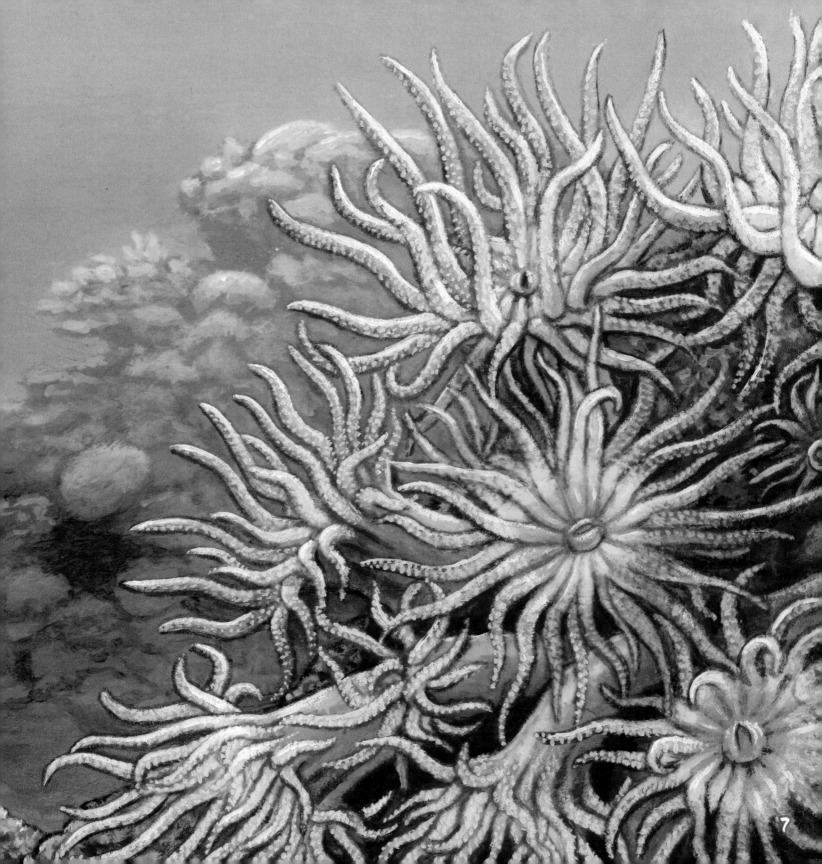

Tiny algae plants hide in the corals. The algae take in the sunlight.

Producers use sunlight, water, nutrients and air to make their own food.

producer

A shrimp crawls along the coral,
searching for food.

consumer,
omnivore

A consumer eats plants or animals for energy.
An omnivore eats both plants and animals.

A green sea turtle swims nearby.
The two animals share a meal of algae.

consumer,
herbivore

 An herbivore eats
only plants.

Swish, swish. A hungry moon wrasse looks for lunch.

With a flick of its tail, the
fish gobbles the shrimp.

consumer,
carnivore

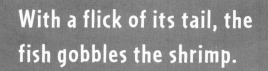
A carnivore eats
only other animals.

consumer,
carnivore

A coral grouper hides out in the coral, waiting. Its wait ends when the moon wrasse swims by.

A huge hunter lurks nearby.
The hungry shark makes its move.

Gulp! The coral grouper is a tasty treat.

consumer, carnivore

17

But even the mighty shark doesn't live forever. Bristle worms and crabs feed on its body.

consumer, scavenger

A scavenger eats mainly dead plants or animals.

Tiny bacteria break down
what's left of the shark.

decomposers

 Decomposers break down dead plants and animals.
Their waste is used as nutrients by plants.

The bacteria turn the shark's body into nutrients. Other sea animals and plants will use the nutrients to grow. And the food chain continues on.

FOOD WEB

Now that you've learned about one food chain, take a look at this food web of the Great Barrier Reef. A food web is made up of many food chains within a single place.

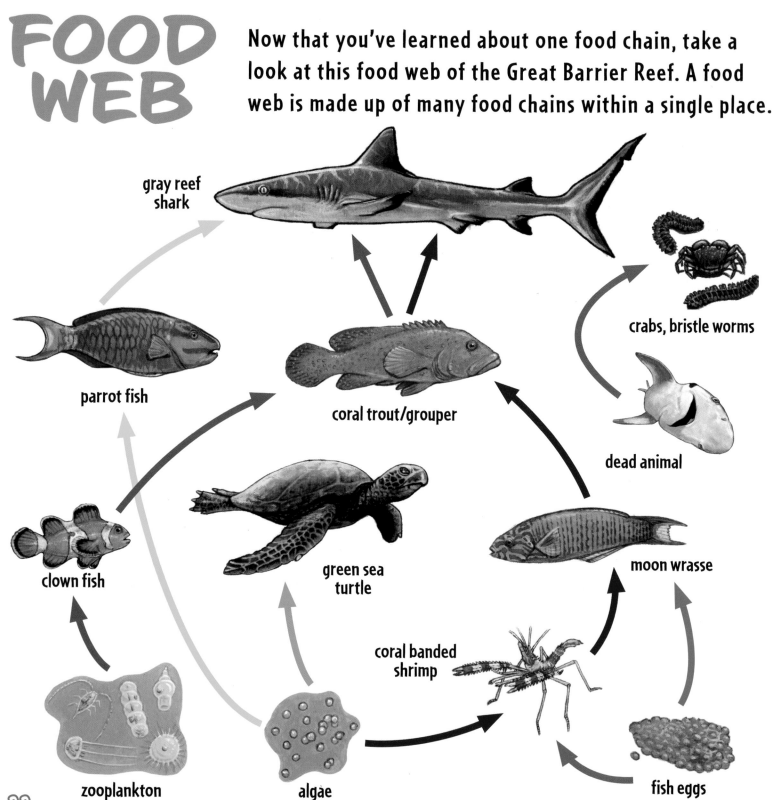

gray reef shark

parrot fish

clown fish

zooplankton

coral trout/grouper

green sea turtle

algae

coral banded shrimp

crabs, bristle worms

dead animal

moon wrasse

fish eggs

GLOSSARY

algae—small plants without roots or stems that grow in water

bacteria—tiny living things that exist all around you and inside you; some bacteria cause disease

carnivore—an animal that eats only other animals

consumer—an animal that eats plants or animals for energy

coral reef—a type of land made up of the hardened bodies of corals; corals are small, colorful sea creatures

decomposer—a living thing, such as fungi or bacteria, that breaks down dead plants or animals

herbivore—an animal that eats only plants

nutrient—a part of food, like a vitamin, that is used for growth

omnivore—an animal that eats both plants and animals

producer—a plant that uses sunlight, water, nutrients, and air to grow

scavenger—an animal that feeds mainly on dead plants or animals

skeleton—the bones that support and protect the body of a human or another animal

READ MORE

Hooks, Gwendolyn. *Makers and Takers: Studying Food Webs in the Ocean.* Studying Food Webs. Vero Beach, Fla.: Rourke Pub., 2009.

Slade Suzanne. *What If There Were No Sea Otters?: A Book about the Ocean Ecosystem.* Food Chain Reactions. Mankato, Minn.: Picture Window Books, 2011.

Wojahn, Rebecca Hogue, and Donald Wojahn. *A Coral Reef Food Chain: A Who-Eats-What Adventure in the Caribbean Sea.* Follow That Food Chain. Minneapolis: Lerner Publications, 2010.

INTERNET SITES

FactHound offers a safe, fun way to find Internet sites related to this book. All of the sites on FactHound have been researched by our staff.

Here's all you do:

Visit *www.facthound.com*

Type in this code: 9781404873858

Super-cool stuff! Check out projects, games and lots more at www.capstonekids.com

INDEX

LOOK FOR ALL THE BOOKS IN THE FOOD CHAINS SERIES:

WHAT EATS WHAT IN A DESERT FOOD CHAIN

WHAT EATS WHAT IN A FOREST FOOD CHAIN

WHAT EATS WHAT IN A RAIN FOREST FOOD CHAIN

WHAT EATS WHAT IN AN OCEAN FOOD CHAIN

Thanks to our advisers for their expertise, research, and advice:
Glenn R. Almany, PhD
ARC Centre of Excellence for Coral Reef Studies
James Cook University, Australia

Terry Flaherty, PhD, Professor of English
Minnesota State University, Mankato

Editor: Shelly Lyons
Designer: Alison Thiele
Art Director: Nathan Gassman
Production Specialist: Danielle Ceminsky
The illustrations in this book were created with Acrylic paint.

Picture Window Books
1710 Roe Crest Drive
North Mankato, MN 56003
www.capstonepub.com

Library of Congress Cataloging-in-Publication Data
Slade, Suzanne.
What eats what in an ocean food chain? / by Suzanne Slade ; illustrations by Zack McLaughlin.
    p. cm.—(Capstone Picture Window Books: food chains)
  Includes index.
ISBN 978-1-4048-7385-8 (library binding)
ISBN 978-1-4048-7696-5 (paperback)
ISBN 978-1-4048-7984-3 (ebook PDF)
1. Marine ecology—Juvenile literature. 2. Marine animals—Juvenile literature. 3. Food chains (Ecology)—Juvenile literature. I. McLaughlin, Zack, ill. II. Title.

QH541.5.S3S538 2013
577.7—dc23   2012001116

Printed in the United States of America in North Mankato, Minnesota.
072014   008276R